THE

CENTENNIAL HISTORY

OF THE

BATTLE OF BENNINGTON;

COMPILED

FROM THE MOST RELIABLE SOURCES, AND FULLY
ILLUSTRATED WITH ORIGINAL DOCUMENTS
AND ENTERTAINING ANECDOTES.

COL. SETH WARNER'S IDENTITY IN THE FIRST ACTION
COMPLETELY ESTABLISHED.

BY

FRANK W. COBURN.

EMBELLISHED WITH A PORTRAIT OF GENERAL STARK, A PLAN OF
THE BATTLE-FIELD, AND OTHER ENGRAVINGS.

"True to its trust, Walloomsack long
The record bright shall bear,
Who came up at the battle sound
And fought for freedom there."
— REV. E. H. CHAPIN, D. D.

BOSTON:
GEORGE E. LITTLEFIELD,
Antiquarian Bookstore, 67 Cornhill.
1877.

BOSTON:
W. F. BROWN & CO., STEREOTYPERS AND PRINTERS,
No. 50 BROMFIELD STREET.

Printing Statement:

Due to the very old age and scarcity of this book,
many of the pages may be hard to read due to the
blurring of the original text, possible missing pages,
missing text, dark backgrounds and other issues
beyond our control.

Because this is such an important and rare work, we
believe it is best to reproduce this book regardless of
its original condition.

Thank you for your understanding.

INTRODUCTION.

In the following pages I have endeavored to present a comprehensive, readable, and above all, a faithful account of the battle fought near Bennington, August 16th, 1777. I have consulted, in the preparation of this work, the Collections of the Vermont and Massachusetts Historical Societies; Records of the Council of Safety of Vermont, edited by E. P. Walton; Slade's Vermont State Papers; Thompson's Vermont; Hemmenway's Vermont Magazine; Isaac Jennings's Memorials of a Century; Nelson's Burgoyne's Campaign; Everett's Life of Stark, and many other authorities, unnecessary to mention here. From these I have made a liberal use of facts.

My thanks are due to Messrs. Geo. E. Littlefield, and Richard D. Child, of Boston; and to Mr. Charles H. Guild, of Somerville, for their kindness in loaning me material of great value, not otherwise easily accessible.

That the work may contain errors, I do not pretend to deny; if it does, they are unknown to me, for I have labored hard to make it correct. Such as it is, I offer it to the people of my native state, Vermont, and to those of New Hampshire and Massachusetts.

FRANK W. COBURN.

SOMERVILLE, MASS., July 10th, 1877.

TO

H. J. M.,

AS A TOKEN

OF MY

HIGHEST ESTEEM.

The Mouth of the River Boquet.

THE BATTLE OF BENNINGTON.

EARLY in the month of May, 1777, General John Burgoyne arrived in Quebec, and at once proceeded to assume command of the army placed there at his disposal. This force consisted of upwards of seven thousand men, British and German, a corps of artillerists, numbering about five hundred, seven hundred rangers, under Col. St. Ledger, two thousand Canadians, whose services as axemen and general camp assistants it was foreseen would be needed, a sufficient number of seamen for manning the transports on the lakes, and on the Hudson, and a body of scouts, to be used in whatever service that might be required. The officers who seconded Burgoyne in this expedition, were all able and excellent in their respective positions. Among these may be mentioned Maj.-Gen.'s Reidesel and Philips, and Brig.-Gen.'s Frazer, Powal, Hamilton, Specht and Goll.

With all due haste Burgoyne marched down Lake Champlain, and on the 21st of June landed his army on the western shore, at the mouth of

the river Boquet. At this place he was joined
by four or five hundred savages, lured by the
promise of a plenty of plunder, together with a
few gaudy presents in hand. Everything must
be done in military exactness and diplomatic pre-
cision with Gen. Burgoyne, and so he proceeded
to address these sons of the forest in a language
no more than half of which was within the scope
of their comprehensions.

"Persuaded that your magnanimity of charac-
"ter, joined to your principles of affection to the
"King, will give me fuller controul over your
"minds than the military rank with which I am
"invested, I enjoin your most serious attention to
"the rules which I hereby proclaim for your in-
"variable observation during the campaign.

"I positively forbid bloodshed, when you are
"not opposed in arms.

"Aged men, women, children, and prisoners,
"must be held sacred from the knife or hatchet,
"even in the time of actual conflict.

"You shall receive compensation for the pris-
"oners you take; but you shall be called to ac-
"count for scalps."

He gave them permission, however, to take the
scalps of the dead, when killed by their fire, and
in actual opposition; "but on no account, or pre-
tence, or subtlety, or prevarication, are they to
be taken from the wounded, or even dying."

"Base, lurking assassins, incendiaries, ravagers,
and plunderers of the country, to whatever army

they may belong, shall be treated with less reserve; but the latitude must be given you by order, and I must be the judge of the occasion." He gave them the privilege to retaliate on the Americans for any acts of barbarity they might commit.

In reply an old chief of the Iroquois said, "With one common assent, we promise a common obedience to all you have ordered, and all you shall order; and may the father of days give you many and success! We have been tried and tempted by the Bostonians; but we have loved our father, and our hatchets have been sharpened upon our affections."

On July 1st the enemy arrived in the immediate vicinity of Ticonderoga, and on the 4th Burgoyne issued his famous proclamation wherein he guarantees his fullest protection to the "domestic, the industrious, the infirm, and even the timid," provided they will "remain quietly at their houses; that they do not suffer their cattle to be removed, nor their corn or forage to be secreted or destroyed; that they do not break up their bridges or roads; nor by any other act, directly or indirectly, endeavor to obstruct the operations of the King's troops, or supply or assist those of the enemy." He wishes for more persuasive terms to give his proclamation a sufficient impression, but at all events "let not people be led to disregard it," at whatever distance they may be from the camp, for, "I have but to give stretch to the Indian forces under my direction, and they amount to thousands, to overtake the hardened enemies of G. Britain and America."

He trusts in the eyes of God and men to stand acquitted for his zeal in denouncing and executing the vengeance of the State on the wilful outcasts who still continue in the "phrenzy of hostility."

On the afternoon of the 5th of July, the ene-. my gained the height of Sugar Hill, or Mount Defiance, as it is now called, which commanded both Fort Ticonderoga and the adjoining post, Mount Independence. These two positions, held by about three thousand Americans, were under the immediate command of General Arthur St. Clair, subject, however, to Gen. Philip Schuyler stationed some miles below, at Fort Edward, on the Hudson.

St. Clair found it necessary to call a council of war to determine on what course to pursue. It was unanimously agreed that the posts were no longer tenable, and therefore an immediate evacuation was decided upon. Early the next morning the troops were put in motion, and at four o'clock, the rear guard, under Col. Francis, succeeded in making good their retreat. Some one, contrary to distinct orders, set fire to a house on Mount Independence, the blaze of which revealed every movement of the Americans to the enemy. This created not a little confusion among our troops, but through the personal exertions of St. Clair, order was finally restored.

Upon arriving at Hubbardton the rear guard, consisting then of three regiments and a few stragglers, was placed under the command of Col. Seth Warner, with orders to remain there until the next morning, to allow those who had fallen behind to come up. This force amounted to twelve hundred men, and included, besides his own, the regiments of Col.'s Francis and Hale.

When General Frazer perceived, in the morning of the evacuation, that the Americans were retiring, he commenced an immediate pursuit. General Reidesel, and most of the Brunswickers were likewise ordered to join and act with Frazer, or separately, as circumstances might warrant.

On the morning of the 7th, they came up with Warner, and a bloody conflict ensued. Col. Hale, with his men, ignominiously fled, leaving the regiments of Francis and Warner to cope with the enemy as best they might. Col. Francis fell in the action, and Warner was forced to once more sound the retreat. The loss of the Americans in this battle was three hundred and twenty-four, in killed, wounded, and prisoners, while the enemy's loss was but one hundred and eighty-three.

Burgoyne, with his main army, still continued on his southward course, using every exertion to open the way from Skenesborough to Fort Edward; but so effectually had the Americans blocked up his way, by various means, that his army was frequently twenty-four hours in advancing one mile. On the 30th of July, Bur-

goyne arrived and fixed his head-quarters at Fort
Edward, which post General Schuyler and his
whole force had evacuated on the 22d, and fled
further south, arriving at Stillwater on the 1st
day of August. Burgoyne's forces were now
employed, from his arrival here, until the 15th of
August, in bringing forward batteaux, provisions,
and ammunition from Fort George, at the foot
of Lake George, to the first or nearest navigable
part of the Hudson, a distance of not more than
fifteen miles. The labor was excessive, more
especially for the European soldiers, whose inex-
perience in this part of warfare rendered them
almost unfit for any use; and so with all the
efforts that Burgoyne could possibly make, he
was soon compelled to admit the alarming scarcity of provisions in his camp. The Americans,
too, in retreating, had taken the greatest pains to
destroy everything that might be of any service
to the enemy, whether it might be in the shape
of food or otherwise. "I have called it a desert
country," said Glick, a German officer, "not only
with reference to its natural sterility, and heaven
knows it was sterile enough, but because of the
pains which were taken, and unfortunately with
too great success, to sweep its few cultivated
spots of all articles likely to benefit the invaders."
And so when the welcome news came that there
was a large store of provisions at Bennington,
news brought in by the Tories, Burgoyne at
once determined to seize that place to supply

his own necessities. He entered upon this pro-
ject with great ardor. "With all the elation of
"his hopes," says the Rev. Isaac Jennings, in his
'Memorials of a Century.' "he fitted out this ex-
"pedition with much care. He selected for its
"nucleus and chief dependence a corps of Ried-
"sell's dismounted dragoons, — the same that
"had behaved so gallantly at Hubbardton, — a
"company of sharpshooters, chosen with care
"from all the regiments, under Capt. Frazer, — a
"most excellent officer; — Peters' corps of Loy-
"alists, to be swelled as they proceeded; a body
"of Canadian rangers; Hanan artillerists with
"two cannon; a hundred and fifty Indians. He
"placed all under the care of Lieut.-Col. Baum, a
"skilled and thoroughly brave German officer.
"To these troops he, after they had proceeded on
"their way a little, added fifty chasseurs." Burgoyne, as might be expected, again found it necessary to add one more to his list of State Documents, a species of composition he particularly
delighted in. As usual, it was drawn up with
the greatest of care, and the minutest attention
to detail. I quote it in full:

Burgoyne's Instructions to Col. Baum.

"The object of your expedition is to try the af-
"fections of the country, to disconcert the coun-
"cils of the enemy, to mount the Reidesel's dra-
"goons, to complete Peters's corps, and to obtain
"large supplies of cattle, horses, and carriages.

"The several corps, of which the enclosed is a
"list, are to be under your command.

"The troops must take no tents, and what lit-
"tle baggage is carried by officers, must be on
"their own bat-horses.

"You are to proceed from Batten Kill, to Aslin-
"ton, and take post there, till the detachment of
"provincials under the command of Capt. Sher-
"wood, shall join you from the southward.

"You are then to proceed to Manchester, where
"you will again take post, so as to secure the pass
"of the mountains on the road from Manchester
"to Rockingham; from thence you will detach
"the Indians and light troops to the northward,
"towards Otter Creek. On their return, and also
"receiving intelligence that no enemy is in force
"upon the Connecticut river, you will proceed by
"the road over the mountains to Rockingham,
"where you will take post. This will be the most
"distant post on the expedition, and must be pro-
"ceeded upon with caution, as you will have the
"defile of the mountains behind you, which might
"make a retreat difficult. You must therefore
"endeavor to be well informed of the force of the
"enemy's militia in the neighboring country.
"Should you find it may with prudence be effect-
"ed, you are to remain there, while the Indians
"and light troops are detached up the river, and
"you are afterwards to descend the river, to Brat-
"tlebury, and from that place, by the quickest
"march, you are to return by the great road to
"Albany.

"During your whole progress, your detach-
"ments are to have orders to bring in to you, all
"horses fit to mount the dragoons, under your
"command; to serve as bat-horses to the troops,

"together with as many saddles and bridles as
"can be found. The number of horses requisite,
"besides those necessary for mounting the reg-
"iment of dragoons, ought to be thirteen hun-
"dred. If you can bring more for the use of the
"army, it will be so much the better. Your par-
"ties are likewise to bring in waggons and other
"convenient carriages, with as many draft-oxen
"as will be necessary to draw them; and all cattle
"fit for slaughter (milch cows excepted), which
"are to be left for the use of the inhabitants.
"Regular receipts, in the form hereto subjoined,
"are to be given in all places where any of the
"above-mentioned articles are taken, to such per-
"sons as have remained in their habitations, and
"otherwise complied with the terms of General
"Burgoyne's Manifesto: but no receipt to be
"given to such as are known to be acting in the
"service of the Rebels. As you will have with
"you persons who are perfectly acquainted with
"the abilities of the country, it may perhaps be
"advisable to tax the several districts, with the
"portions of the several articles, and limit the
"hours of delivery; and should you find it neces-
"sary to move before the delivery can be made,
"hostages of the most respectable people should
"be taken, to secure their following you the ensu-
"ing day. All possible measures to be used to
"prevent plundering. As it is probable that Capt.
"Sherwood, who is already detached to the south-
"ward, and will join you at Arlington, will drive
"a considerable quantity of horses and cattle in to
"you, you will therefore send in this cattle to the
"army, with a proper detachment from Peters's
"corps, to cover them, in order to disincumber
"yourself; but you must always keep the regi-

"ment of dragoons compact. The dragoons
"themselves must ride and take care of the
"horses of the regiment. Those horses which are
"destined for the army must be tied together by
"strings of ten each, in order that one man may
"lead ten horses. You will give the unarmed
"men of Peters's corps to conduct them, and in-
"habitants whom you can trust. You must always
"take your camps in good position, but at the
"same time where there is pasture, and you must
"have a chain of sentinels around your horses
"and cattle when grazing. Col. Skeene will be
"with you as much as possible, in order to assist
"you with his advice, to help you to distinguish
"the good subjects from the bad, to procure you
"the best intelligence of the enemy, and to choose
"those people who are to bring me the accounts
"of your progress and success.

"When you find it necessary to halt for a day
"or two, you must always entrench the camp of
"the regiment of Dragoons, in order never to
"risque an attack or affront from the enemy.

"As you will return with the regiment of dra-
"goons mounted, you must always have a detach-
"ment of Capt. Frazer's or Peters's corps in front
"of the column, and the same in the rear, in order
"to prevent your falling into an ambuscade, when
"you march through the woods.

"You will use all possible means to make the
"enemy believe that the troops under your com-
"mand are the advanced corps of the army, and
"that it is intended to pass the Connecticut on
"the road to Boston.

"You will likewise insinuate that the main
"army from Albany is to be joined at Springfield
"by a corps of troops from Rhode Island. It is

"highly probable that the corps under Mr. War-
"ner, now supposed to be at Manchester, will
"retreat before you; but should they, contrary to
"expectation, be able to collect in great force, and
"post themselves advantageously, it is left to your
"discretion to attack them or not, always bearing
"in mind that your corps is too valuable to let
"any considerable loss be hazarded on this occa-
"sion.

  "Should any corps be moved from Mr. Arnold's
"main army, in order to intercept your retreat,
"you are to take as strong a post as the country
"will afford, and send the quickest intelligence
"to me, and you may depend on my making such
"a movement as shall put the enemy between two
"fires, or otherwise effectually sustain you.

  "It is imagined that the whole of this expedi-
"tion may be effected in about a fortnight, but
"every movement of it must depend upon your
"success in obtaining such supply of provisions
"as will enable you to subsist for your return to
"the army, in case you get no more; and should
"not the army be able to reach Albany before
"your expedition shall be completed, I will find
"means to give you notice of it, and give your
"rout another direction.

  "All persons acting in committees, or any offi-
"cers under the directions of the Congress, either
"civil or military, are to be made prisoners.

  "I heartily wish you success, and have the
"honor to be, Sir,

        "Your most obedient humble servant,

            "J. BURGOYNE, *Lieutenant-General.*
  "HEAD-QUARTERS, August 9th, 1777.

It will be seen that the above document is

dated August 9th, 1877, but it was not until the early morning of the 12th that Baum left for Bennington. The great object, as expressed in his instructions, was to obtain horses and cattle, but when his departure drew near at hand, the consideration of provisions arose, and so these same instructions were modified a little.

That afternoon, at four o'clock, they arrived at the Batten Kill, and encamped. It was at this place that the fifty chasseurs overtook them, that Burgoyne had sent out as a reinforcement. At five the next morning, Baum again moved forward towards Cambridge, sending ahead a force of thirty provincials and fifty Indians to surprise an American army-guard, with some cattle, that he had heard were stationed there, which succeeded in capturing five prisoners. Arriving at Cambridge, Baum captured a number of horses, cattle, wagons and carts, and then sent word back to Burgoyne as to his progress, and the success he had met with, not forgetting to inform him, also, that it had been rumored there were at least eighteen hundred men assembled at Bennington, ready to receive him. Upon receiving this communication, Burgoyne replied as follows:

General Burgoyne to Lieutenant-Colonel Baum.

"Near Saratoga, 14 August, 1777."

" Sir,"

" The accounts you have given me are very sat-
"isfactory, and I doubt not every proceeding un-

"der your direction will be the same. I beg the
"favor of you to report whether the route you
"have marched will be practicable with a large
"corps of cannon, without repair, or with what
"sort of repair. The desirable circumstances for
"your corps is, at present, to possess Bennington;
"but should you find the enemy too strongly
"posted, and maintaining such a countenance as
"would make a *coup de main* hazardous, I wish
"you to take such a post as you can maintain till
"you hear further from me; and upon your re-
"ports and other circumstances, I will either sup-
"port you in force or withdraw you.

"You will please send to my camp, as soon as
"you can, wagons and draught-cattle, and like-
"wise such other cattle as are not necessary for
"your subsistence. Let the wagons and carts
"bring off what flour and wheat they can, that
"you do not retain for the same purpose. I will
"write to you in full to-morrow in regard to pur-
"chasing horses out of the hands of the savages.
"In the meantime let them be assured that what-
"ever you select from them, fit to mount the dra-
"goons, shall be paid for at proper price.

"I am, &c.,

"JOHN BURGOYNE."

To aid Baum, in case he needed it, General
Burgoyne, at 8 o'clock on the 15th day of August,
ordered Col. Breyman with a large force, consisting of a company of yagers, and a battalion of
chasseurs and grenadiers to follow and act as a
re-enforcement. He had himself moved the main
army down the east bank of the Hudson, and the

advanced corps succeeded in crossing over on a bridge of rafts, and encamped near Saratoga. The difficulty Breyman's troops experienced in crossing the Batten Kill, the muddy roads and rainy weather, prevented them from reaching Cambridge that day, and so they encamped seven miles from that place. He had, before reaching the night's encampment, despatched an express to Col. Baum, informing him of his proposed assistance, the reply to which he received the next morning.

The progress of the invading army had been watched with a great deal of interest by the inhabitants through whose territory it passed. The alarm spread rapidly far into New York, and on the other side, even beyond the Green Mountains to the Connecticut river. The spirit that governed the people was generally one of bitter opposition, although many submissively took the oath of allegiance for the sake of protecting their families, it was alleged, but the truth is they were inspired more by cowardice than any of the benefits of policy. Some of these were loud in their denunciations of the course pursued by the Parliament of Great Britain, but when the opportunity came to vindicate their opinions, it was discovered that they "did not believe in war"; that they had rather submit to "trifling wrongs" than to "take up arms against their brothers." Tender consideration! Burgoyne found, much to his dismay, and by bitter experience, that these people existed in a small minority. He had flattered himself that his "Proclamations" would at once convince the greater portion of the inhabitants the needlessness of rebellion, the folly of any kind of opposition, the sublime mercy of the King! This mistake did not fully dawn upon his mind at once, but required the battle of Bennington to develop. In a private letter to Lord George Germain, dated August 20th, 1877, he says, "Wherever the King's forces point, militia to the amount of three or four thousand assemble in twenty-four hours; they bring with them their subsistence, etc., and the alarm over, they return to their farms. The Hampshire Grants, in particular, a country unpeopled, and almost unknown in the last war, now abounds in the most active and most rebellious race of the continent, and hangs like a gathering storm on my left." That there were some actuated by what they considered to be right motives, none can doubt. They made sacrifices to sustain what they deemed to be principles. Their estates in Vermont were sold to meet the expences of an armed force to oppose them in the field. They might have hoped to regain them at some future day, but still it was, at least, the risk of a sacrifice.

The people who preferred to stand on the side of the American cause were not without their troubles and dangers. Those of them residing in the northern parts of the Grants, and in some parts of New York, were compelled to move their

worldly goods farther south in order to prevent
them from falling into the hands of the enemy.
Those residing in the south gladly received them
and shared with them the hospitality of their
roofs.   They were willing, indeed, to share with
each other their "mutual cares, labors and dangers."

In order to meet Burgoyne with something like
a show of spirited opposition, the Vermont Council of Safety, a body appointed by the Convention
that formed the Vermont Constitution to act until the new government could be organized, called
upon New Hampshire and Massachusetts to aid
in the defence of the frontier, urging, as a reason
for their immediate action, that in case Vermont
was neglected, the war would of necessity be carried into their own territory.

ADDRESS OF THE COUNCIL OF SAFETY IN VERMONT, TO
THE COUNCILS OF SAFETY IN MASSACHUSETTS AND NEW
HAMPSHIRE.

*"In Council of Safety, State of Vermont, Man-
chester, July* 15, 1777.

" GENTLEMEN : This state, in particular, seems
" to be at present the object of destruction.   By
" the surrender of the fortress of Ticonderoga,
" a communication is opened to the defenceless
" inhabitants on the frontier, who, having little
" more in store at present, than sufficient for the
" maintenance of their respective families, and not
" ability immediately to remove their effects, are,
" therefore, induced to accept such protections as

"are offered them by the enemy. By this means,
"those towns who are most contiguous to them,
"are under the necessity of taking such protec-
"tion; by which the next town or towns become
"equally a frontier as the former towns, before
"such protection; and unless we can have the as-
"sistance of our friends, so as to put it immediately
"in our power to make a sufficient stand against
"such strength as they may send, it appears that
"it will soon be out of the power of this state to
"maintain its territory.

"This country, notwithstanding its infancy,
"seems to be as well supplied with provisions for
"victualling an army as any on the continent; so
"that on that account we cannot see why a stand
"may not as well be made in this state as in the
"Massachusetts; and more especially, as the in-
"habitants are disposed to defend their liberties.

"You, gentlemen, will be at once sensible, that
"every such town as accepts protection, is ren-
"dered at that instant incapable of affording any
"further assistance; and what is infinitely worse,
"as some disaffected persons eternally lurk in al-
"most every inhabited town, such become doubly
"fortified to injure their country, our good dispo-
"sition to defend ourselves, and make a frontier
"for your state with our own, which cannot be
"carried into execution without your assistance.
"Should you send immediate assistance, we can
"help you; and should you neglect till we are put
"to the necessity of taking protection, you know
"it is in a moment out of our power to assist you.
"Your laying these circumstances together will, I
"hope, induce your honours to take the same into
"consideration, and immediately send us your de-
"termination in the premises. I have the satisfac-

"tion to be, your honours most obedient and very
"humble servant, by order of council."

"IRA ALLEN, Sec'ry."

The state of New Hampshire replied as follows:

LETTER FROM MESCHECH WEARE, PRESIDENT OF THE STATE
OF NEW HAMPSHIRE, TO IRA ALLNE, SECRETARY OF
THE STATE OF VERMONT.

"EXETER, JULY 19, 1777.

"SIR: I was favoured with yours of the 15th
"inst. yesterday by express, and laid the same be-
"fore our general court, who are sitting.

"We had, previous thereto, determined to send
"assistance to your state. They have now deter-
"mined, that a quarter part of the militia of twelve
"regiments shall be immediately draughted, formed
"into three battalions, under the command of Brig.
"Gen. John Stark, and forthwith sent into your
"state, to oppose the ravages and coming forward
"of the enemy; and orders are now issuing, and
"will all go out in a few hours, to the several
"Colonels for that purpose. Dependence is made
"that they will be supplied with provision in your
"state; and I am to desire your convention will
"send some proper person or persons to Number
"Four, by Thursday next, to meet Gen. Stark
"there, and advise with him relative to the route
"and disposition of our troops, and to give him
"such information as you may then have, relative
"to the manœuvres of the enemy. In behalf of
"the council and assembly, I am, sir, your most
"obedient humble servant,"

"MESCHECH WEARE, President."

"IRA ALLEN, ESQ., <i>Secretary of the State of Vermont.</i>"

Col. John Stark had retired from the service of the Continental Army for the particular reason that Congress in making out a new list of promotions, had omitted his name, and advanced others, whom, he considered, if not in rank, at least in ability, every way his inferiors. His experience among the Indians, and his valuable services in the French War, had endeared him to the respect of the citizens of New Hampshire, and in thus retiring from the army, he had many sympathisers.

Stark was one of the first to start for the sea-coast, upon hearing of the affair at Lexington and Concord. He had left instructions for such as desired to follow him as volunteers in the cause of the Colonists, to rendezvous at Medford, a small town four or five miles from Boston. About twelve hundred men obeyed his call, although some of these returned home on discovering that the pursuit of military glory was not without its attendant danger. These men were formed into two regiments, and Stark received his commission as Colonel of what was known as the First New Hampshire. This regiment served with considerable credit at the battle of Bunker Hill, more properly Breed's Hill, where they occupied a position on the left wing of the American lines of defence. They came out of the action with a loss of sixty in killed and wounded.

Colonel Stark and his men followed the fortunes of the army until the time of the regimental enlistment had expired. He succeeded, however, in getting them to remain for a brief period, and hastened himself to New Hampshire, to recruit others for the service.   It was while engaged in this laudable enterprise, that the news came to him of the omission of his name on the new promotion list.   Disappointed and almost angry, he sent in his resignation, and returned to his farm, to follow the avocations of a peaceful life.   His letter addressed to the New Hampshire Council, fully expresses his feelings at that time.

" *To the Honb'l the Council and House of Repre-*
"*sentatives for the State of New Hampshire in*
"*General Court assembled.*"

"Ever since hostilities commenced, I have as
"in me lay, endeavoured to prevent my Country
"from being ravaged and enslaved by our cruel
"and unnatural Enemy, have undergone the hard-
"ships and fatigues of two campaigns with cheer-
"fulness and alacrity, ever enjoying the pleasing
"satisfaction that I was doing my God and my
"country the greatest service my abilities would
"admit of, and it was with the utmost gratitude
"that I accepted the important command to which
"this State appointed me.   I should have served
"with the greatest pleasure, more especially at
"this important crisis, when our Country calls for
"the utmost exertions of every American, but am
"extremely grieved that I feel bound in honor to
"leave the service, Congress having thought fit
"to promote junior officers over my head, so that
"I should show myself unworthy the honor con-
"ferred on me, and a want of that spirit which
"should glow in the breast of every officer ap-

"pointed by this Honorable House, in not suita-
"bly resenting an indignity. I must, (though
"grieved to leave the service of my Country,) beg
"leave to resign my commission, hoping that you
"will make a choice of some gentleman who may
"honor the cause and his country to succeed.

"Your most obedient
"and much obliged humble servant,
"JOHN STARK."

The Council passed the following vote, March
21st, 1777.

"Voted, that the thanks of both houses in the
"convention, be given to Col. Stark, for his good
"services in the present war, and from his early
"and steadfast attachments to the cause of his
"country, they make not the least doubt that his
"future conduct in whatever state of life Provi-
"dence may place him, will manifest the same no-
"ble disposition of mind."

In response to Vermont's call for aid, the Assembly of New Hampshire formed the whole
State Militia into two brigades, giving the command of the first to William Whipple, and of the
second to John Stark. In accepting this command, Stark had hesitated, still smarting under
the neglect of the Continental Congress. Upon
being assured that his name was a power in itself
among the soldiers, and above all, upon being
urged to accept as a duty he owed to his country, he could no longer resist the offer. He accepted, however, on the condition that he should
not be responsible to the Continental Congress,

nor to any officers acting under that honorable body, but to only the New Hampshire Assembly. His terms were readily agreed to, and he went at once to work.

"STATE OF NEW HAMPSHIRE,
"*Saturday, July 19th,* 1777.

"To Brig^d Genl Jno Stark,—You are hereby "required to repair to Charlestown, No. 4, so as "to be there by the 24th—Thursday next, to "meet and confer with persons appointed by the "Convention of the State of Vermont, relative to "the route of the Troops under your Command, "their being supplied with Provisions, and future "operations—and when the Troops are collected "at No. 4, you are to take the command of them "and march into the State of Vermont, and there "act in conjunction with the Troops of that State, "or any other of the States, or of the United "States, or separately, as it shall appear Expe- "dient to you for the protection of the People or "the annoyance of the Enemy, and from time to "time, as occasion shall require, send Intelligence "to the Genl Assembly or Committee of Safety, "of your operations, and the manœuvres of the "Enemy.　　　　　"M. WEARE."

Col. Warner, now stationed at Manchester, was using his every exertion to collect troops for im- mediate service. In his circular for aid, issued to the commanders of the militia in Hampshire and Worcester Counties in Massachusetts, he says, "The number of Troops we have at present "collected, don't exceed 500, and unless we have "speedy help, (should the enemy approach,) we

"must be obliged to retreat before them, and leave
"them to possess a great part of what we have.
"You may conclude the Frontiers will be where
"there is a Body of Troops sufficient to stand the
"ememy. All are desired to bring Kettles and
"utensils for Cooking." To Stark, from the same
place, he wrote: "I can, by no means, be able
"to make a stand, without assistance. It is there-
"fore, of the most pressing importance, that your
"troops be forwarded to this place with as much
"expedition as possible. . . . The Council of
"Safety of this State are present, and join me in
"urging the necessity of your speedy assistance."

General Stark, agreeably to the orders of the
Assembly, had stationed himself at No. 4, and in
response to Colonel Warner's request, had on the
28th of July, sent a body of men numbering two
hundred and fifty, to his aid, and again on the 30th
another detachment, at the same time promising
more as they came in. He remained at this place
until August 3rd, then leaving for Manchester.
August 6th, he arrived in Bromley, now known as
Peru, and on the next day he reached the head-
quarters of Warner at Manchester. The number
of troops he had forwarded, amounted, altogether,
to eight hundred men, and he found assembled at
Manchester, about six hundred more, making uni-
tedly, fourteen hundred. Brigadier-General Stark
was met here by Maj.-Gen. Lincoln, with instructions for him to join the main force of the Americans under Schuyler, on the Hudson. This Stark

positively refused to do, on the grounds that the best way to defeat Burgoyne's purpose, was not to oppose him with small forces in the front, but to hang upon his rear, and by continually cutting off his supplies, so embarrass his movements, as to finally disarrange his plans. General Lincoln communicated what he deemed to be Stark's insubordination, to his superior, General Schuyler, and also to Congress. Stark had shown under what authority he was acting; endeavored to explain that as he was working for the State of New Hampshire, and that State alone; that he could not possibly consider himself responsible to the United States, and more especially as his commission expressly stated that his responsibility went no farther than that, he deemed himself as inferior in command to no military officer. He should be very glad, he said, to confer with General Schuyler as to the best way to meet the enemy; possibly something, better than had as yet been suggested, might be done, but, he continued, I never can join General Schuyler to act as a subordinate. The result of this was, that on the 19th of August, three days after the battle of Bennington, and some time before they heard of it, Congress voted, "that a copy of General Lincoln's "letter be forthwith transmitted to the Council of "New Hampshire, and that they be informed that "the instructions, which General Stark says he "received from them, are destructive of military "subordination, and highly prejudicial to the com-

"mon cause at this crisis; and that therefore they
"be desired to instruct General Stark to conform
"himself to the same rules, which other General
"officers of the militia are subject to, whenever
"they are called out at the expense of the United
"States."

Stark, with ten or twelve hundred men, reached
Bennington, August 9th. This force consisted
partly of New Hampshire, and partly of Vermont
troops, the militia from the eastern side of the
mountains, being under the command of Colonel
William Williams. The only force left at Manchester, was Warner's regiment under Lieutenant
Colonel Samuel Safford. Warner, himself, had
deemed it for the best to go forward with Stark,
as his knowledge of the country around Bennington, might be of valuable assistance to him, and indeed, so it proved.

The activity of the Council of Safety could not
fail to instil a certain degree of enthusiasm in the
minds of all interested in the loyal cause of the
Americans. Every day witnessed the arrival of
new recruits in Bennington, and although many
came unarmed and even unprovided with camp
utensils, these deficiences were supplied as far as
lay in the power of the Council. Uniforms were
entirely unknown in the ranks of the volunteers.
Each one suited his own taste and ability in cloth-
ing himself, and these generally resulted in the
simple farmer's frock and pantaloons. Each one,
also, was expected to furnish his own firearms,

which was readily done, as every man in those days, deemed a gun as one of the first implements of necessity. Cooking utensils were what were lacking most in the camp at Bennington. The little experience of the militia in camp life, had not, as yet, taught them the use of these articles, and so in leaving home they had been overlooked and forgotten. It may be, some thought of them, but deemed them as too much of a luxury to be troubled with their transportation over the mountains and along the dusty roads.

Cattle and provisions for the army were daily arriving. These were seized from the tories, or purchased with the money seized goods brought under the process of a forced sale. The Council had rightly deemed the property of disaffected persons as the proper source of support, as far as it might go, of the militia, and accordingly committees were appointed to turn such property into a state for immediate use.

Commission of Sequestration from the Council.

"In Council of Safety, State of Vermont.
"Bennington, 28th July, 1777.
"To ———: You are hereby required, (agree-
"able to a previous resolve of this Council,) to
"seize all lands, tenements, goods, and chattels,
"of any person or persons in this state, whom you
"know, or may hereafter learn, to have repaired
"to the enemy, and a true inventory thereof to
"take, and return to this Council, except articles
"as are wanted for the use of the army; which

"are wanted at Manchester or elsewhere, where
"there is a contractor to receive and pay for them.
"You will appoint three persons noted for good
"judgment, who are, after being duly sworn, to
"apprize the same ; and all other movable effects
"you are to sell at public vendue, except such
"necessaries as humanity requires for the support
"of such families. And after paying necessary
"charges, you are to remit the remainder of the
"money to this Council. You will take the nat-
"ural and artificial marks of every creature you
"shall receive or take, and their age, from whom
"they came, for what sold, and to whom sold.
"You are to lease out all such lands and tene-
"ments, at a reasonable price, not exceeding two
"years, giving the preference to such persons as
"have been drove from their farms by this war.
"You are further authorized to arrest any person,
"or persons, you shall have sufficient grounds to
"believe are enemies to this and the United States
"of America, and all such persons as you shall
"arrest, you will seize all their movable effects,
"(where there is danger of their being embezzled,)
"and keep in safe custody, until after trial. If
"they are acquitted, to give unto such person or
"persons, such seizour; but if found guilty, to
"make return to the Council. You are to call
"to your assistance, such person or persons as you
"shall find necessary, keeping regular accounts of
"all your procedures."
    "By Order of Council,
            "IRA ALLEN, *Sec'y.*"

This resolution of the Council was obeyed to
the letter. The ones appointed to act as commis-
sioners, were chosen for their upright patriotism,

and well-known enthusiasm, and in executing the laws of the civil authority, they often took an un-usual pleasure as they came in contact with those neighbors and formerly *friends*, separated by opin-ions, a separation often bitter in the extreme.

Thus it was that Colonel Samuel Herrick's reg-iment of Rangers was raised and supported, and thus it was that the other incidental expenses of the common defense were met in Vermont. In New Hampshire, the forces called out to serve under Stark and Whipple, were supported by private loans, for the public treasury was long since empty. John Langdon, a merchant of Portsmouth, and Speaker of the Assembly, was among the foremost in reviving the public courage, at a time when the outlook for the future looked anything but bright and promising. He said, " I "have three thousand dollars in hard money; I "will pledge my plate for three thousand more; " I have seventy hogsheads of Tobago rum, which "shall be sold for the most it will bring. These "are at the service of the state. If we succeed in "defending our firesides and homes, I may be re-"munerated; if we do not, the property will be of "no value to me. Our old friend, Stark, who so "nobly maintained the honor of our state, at Bun-"ker's Hill, may safely be intrusted with the con-"duct of the enterprise, and we will check the "progress of Burgoyne." This proposition infused new life into the Assembly, and no trouble was experienced in raising the two brigades.

Stark, on arriving in Bennington, hardly knew whether to remain there, or proceed at once to the Hudson to oppose Burgoyne in his southward career. It was not until the 13th, that he, learning of the advance of a body of Indians, as far as Cambridge, dispatched Lieut.-Col. Gregg, with two hundred men, to oppose them. On the morning of the 14th, Colonel Baum reached Van Schaik's mills, and found there Colonel Gregg's force in possession. Gregg was forced to retreat before a superior number. Baum, in his letter to Burgoyne, thus relates the affair.

"Sancoik, Aug. 14, 1777, 9 o'clock."

"Sir: I have the honor to inform your Excel-
"lency that I arrived here at eight in the morning,
"having had intelligence of a party of the enemy
"being in the possession of a mill, which they
"abandoned at our approach, but in their usual
"way, fired from the bushes, and took the road to
"Bennington. A savage was slightly wounded.
"They broke down the bridge, which has retarded
"our march about an hour. They left in the mill,
"about seventy-eight barrels of very fine flour, one
"thousand bushels of wheat, twenty barrels of
"salt, and about one thousand pounds worth of
"pearl and pot ashes. I have ordered thirty pro-
"vincials and an officer to guard the provisions
"and the pass of the bridge. By five prisoners
"here, they agree that fifteen hundred to eighteen
"hundred men are in Bennington, but are sup-
"posed to leave it on our approach. I will proceed
"so far to-day, as to fall on the enemy to-morrow
"early, and make such disposition as I think nec-

"essary, from the intelligence I may receive.   Peo-
"ple are flocking in hourly, and want to be armed.
" The savages cannot be controlled, they ruin and
" take everything they please
            " I am, etc.,   " F. Baum."
" To General Burgoyne."

" Beg your Excellency to pardon the hurry of
" this letter; it is written on the head of a barrel."

The Council of Safety, on learning of Baum's
approach, addressed the Colonels of the state militia a circular, urging them to assemble with all
haste at Bennington.

Vermont Council of Safety to the Colonels of the
State Militia.
        " State of Vermont, in Council of Safety."
        " Bennington, 13th Aug., 1777.
" Dear Col.—By Express, this day, received from
" the Commanding officer of the Northern De-
"partment, we Learn that a Door has now opened
"for the Troops of this State to do Duty on this
"side the North River, which will be clear from
" Gen. Schuyler's Command, and as an Expedition
" is on foot, of the greatest importance, which is
" to remain a secret till the Troops are Collected,
" these are therefore the most Positive terms to
" require you, without a moment's Loss of Time,
" to march one half of the Regiment under your
" Command, to this Place.   No small excuse at
" this Juncture can be received.
" Whilst I am writing this, we are informed by
" Express, that a Large Body of the Enemy's troops
" were discovered two hours ago, in St. Koik, 12
" miles from this Place, and another Body at Cam-

"bridge, About 18 miles from this, that they
"marched Boldly in the Road, and there will
"Doubtless, be an Attack at or near this place,
"within 24 howers. We have the assistance of
"Maj.-general Stark with his Brigade. You will
"hurry what Rangers forward are Recruted, with
"all speed. Now is the Time, Sr.

I am, Sʳ, your Humble Servant.

"Sr, I Desire you would, By order of Council,
"Send this Express to General Baley, Peter Ol-
"cott, Col., Colº. Marsh.

JONAS FAY, *Vice President.*

"TO MAJ. ISRAEL SMITH, OF STRAFFORD."

Although the Americans under Gregg had retreated and left Baum in full possession of the
field at Sancoik, yet that officer began to lose
that easy confidence and egotistical self-assurance
he had formerly experienced. Trained in the
military school of Burgoyne, he had learned to
look down on the sturdy farmers of New York,
and the New England States, regarding them as
extremely rustic in all that pertained to military
knowledge and experience. And yet Baum, while
he held in contempt the Americans as soldiers, had
the simplicity to believe in their general loyalty to
King George, proving again the thoroughness of
Burgoyne's teaching. He allowed the people to
go and come to and from his camp, readily believ-
ing their professions of smypathy with the royal
cause, and imparting to them most fully and completely all information as to his strength and designs. This course, it seems, did not meet with

the approval of his subordinates. They believed he was wrong in trusting to the country people to such an extent as he had done. They believed, many of them, that concealed beneath the plain manners and open countenances of the visitors, there was a keenness and avidity in collecting facts, and that under the guise of simple questions and a careless listening to the answers, valuable information was being intentionally sought for and too readily obtained. These simple inquirers might be earnest and thoughtful ones! One of his own officers, in his account of the expedition, says of Baum, " He considered all persons sincere who professed attachment to the royal cause; alluding in their presence, and without reserve, both to his own numbers and designs; and as by far the greater portion were in reality traitors to us, every circumstance connected with our dispositions and plans became as well known to the enemy as to ourselves."

As Gregg retreated from Sancoik, he caused the bridge to be destroyed, which so delayed Baum, who had started in pursuit, that his force retired unmolested. "The Americans," says Glick, "though they gave way at last, fought like men conscious of their own prowess, and confident of the strength of the support which was behind them; and this, coupled with the rumors which had reached us relative to the amount of the garrison at Bennington, failed not to startle both Col. Baum and the boldest of his troops." So much time was occupied in repairing the bridge, that Baum despaired of reaching Bennington that night, and so he encamped but a few miles from Sancoik, at Walloomsac.

Stark, on the night of the 13th, having learned more completely as to the opposition Col. Gregg was to meet with, determined to march with what force could be immediately commanded, to his assistance. On the morning of the 14th, he rallied his brigade and what militia was at Bennington and in the neighborhood; sent to Manchester for the remnant of Warren's regiment; left definite orders for such volunteers as should come in, to join him at once, and then marched to meet the enemy. Some five or six miles on the way he met Col. Gregg retreating before Baum. Here Stark drew up his line of battle, expecting naturally enough, to be attacked; but Baum preferred to halt on a hill or advantageous rise of ground, and then Stark retired a mile or two to develop more mature plans. Before doing so, however, he killed or wounded thirty of the enemy without the loss of a single man. After halting, this the second time, a council was called, and it was agreed to attack the enemy on the following day, but on the 15th it rained, so that nothing more was accomplished, otherwise than a few skirmishes. Baum occupied the day in strengthening his defenses on the heights of the Walloomsac.

The farm of Walloomsac lay upon both sides of the river, and consisting at that time of farm buildings to the extent of six or eight log huts, scattered here and there over a narrow expanse of cultivated ground. The position chosen by Baum lay at the west of the river, on an elevation admirably adapted for a vigorous defense. Here he stationed the dragoons with a portion of the workmen on the right in the rear of a little zig-zag breastwork composed of logs and loose earth. Such of the log huts as came within his lines he filled with Canadians, supporting them with chasseurs and grenadiers, also entrenched behind breastworks. Baum's whole force, with the exception of about one hundred men, were on the west side of the river. The road in his flank was held by the Indians. According to the map of Lieutenant Durnford, Colonel Baum's engineer, a corps of Reidesel's dragoons and a number of Canadian Rangers were stationed behind the breastworks; some paces in advance a little down the declivity towards the river was another corps of Reidesel's dragoons; still further down, at the foot of the hill near the bend of the river, a body of chasseurs; by the river, to the right, near the bridge and on both sides of the road, miner fortifications defended by Canadian Rangers and German Grenadiers; nearly south of the principal fortifications, another body of Grenadier and Tories; and over the river, on a little rise of ground, still other fortifications defended by tories under the immediate command of Col. Pfister, as he was popularly known, a retired British Lieutenant of the French War. This position was nearly south-east of Baum's principal line of defense, which was situated on the top of a hill rising three or four hundred feet above the Walloomsac, which flows here nearly south. The road from Bennington to Cambridge, runs, after crossing the river at right angles, nearly westward, touching the base of the hill.

Baum occupied the entire day of the 15th in completing the defenses, nor was his work finished with the setting of the sun, but lasted far into the night. He had become really anxious as to the results of the morrow, and this anxiety was shared very generally throughout his whole camp. "There we passed the night," says Glick, "not very comfortably, as may well be supposed, seeing that no fires were lighted, and that we were all impressed with a powerful sense of impending danger. . . . There were few amongst us that slept very soundly. We could not but remember that we were cut off, by a wide tract of desolate country, from all communications with our friends, and exposed to attacks on every side from a numerous enemy; and the whoop which the savages raised from time to time, as well as the occasional musket shot, gave notice, that even now that enemy was not inactive. Our anxiety for the return of day was greater by far than perhaps any of us would have been willing to acknowledge, even to his dearest friend." Baum, feeling the need of reinforcements, dispatched a messenger to Col. Breyman, stationed at the Batten Kill, asking that officer to come to his aid at once.

The rain falling so heavily on the 15th, prevented Stark from making any general attack on the principal line of defense, but small parties were kept out actively skirmishing, much to the annoyance of the enemy. In the meantime, the Council of Safety was not idle. Messengers were dispatched for ammunition to all quarters where it was likely to be found.

"STATE OF VERMONT,
Bennington.—In Council of Safety, Aug. 15, 1777.

"SIR—You are hereby desired to forward to "this place, by express, all the lead you can pos-"sibly collect in your vicinity; as it is expected "every minute, an action will commence between "our troops and the enemies', within four or five "miles of this place, and the lead will be positive-"ly wanted. By order of Council,

"PAUL SPOONER, *D. Sec'y.*

"The Chairman of the Committee of Safety, "Williamstown.

"The same request sent to the Chairman of the "Committee, Lanesboro, the same date, sent by "Jedediah Reed, Paulett.

"Madam—Please to send by the bearer, Jede-"diah Reed, 6 or 7 lbs. of lead, by Col. Simonds' "order. By order of Council,

"PAUL SPOONER, *D. Sec'y.*
"MRS. SIMONDS."

Before daylight on the morning of the 16th, Stark was reinforced by a small body of militia, under Colonel Simonds from Berkshire county, Massachusetts. Among them was the Reverend Thomas Allen, of Pittsburg, whose warlike ardor was of the most glowing kind. He was with Gen. St. Clair at the evacuation of Forts Ticonderoga and Mt. Independence, and always expressed a great contempt for the quiet surrender of those posts. He would say, that had he commanded there, the ramparts, though carried at last, would have first been baptized in blood. Subsequent to the battle of Bennington, speaking of the outlook for America's future, he writes, "A short time will decide the fate of America. It must depend on the treatment of those five general officers who gave up Ticonderoga. . . . . If these cannot be brought to justice, than I am ready to pronounce what is, in my opinion, the sad doom of these States — the end is come!" He had taken an active part in rallying the Berkshire militia at the urgent call of General Stark, knowing well that where Stark was, there would be at least *fighting*, whatever the result might be.

It was during a drenching shower, that this force reached the vicinity of the American camp, and though wet to the skin, Mr. Allen sought the General's headquarters.

"General Stark," said Allen, "the Berkshire militia have often been summoned to the field, without being allowed to fight; now if you don't give them a chance this time, they will never turn out again."

Stark smilingly asked, " Do you wish to march now while it is dark and raining?"

" No, not just at this moment," was the reply.

" Well, then," said the General, "if the Lord will give us sunshine in the morning, and I do not give you fighting enough, I will never ask you to come out again."

And when the morning sun arose, hardly a cloud was seen in the heavens, and, to use the words of Glich, who was present, " the very leaves hung mo-" tionless, and the long grass waved not under the " influence of a perfect calm. Every object around, " too, appeared to peculiar advantage; for the " fields looked green and refreshed, the river was " swollen and tumultuous, and the branches were " all loaded with dew-drops, which glittered in the " sun's early rays, like so many diamonds. Nor " would it be easy to imagine any scene more rife " with peaceful and even pastoral beauty. Look-" ing down from this summit of the rising ground, " I beheld immediately beneath me a wide sweep of " stately forest, interrupted at remote intervals by " green meadows or yellow corn-fields, whilst here " and there a cottage, a shed, or some other primi-" tive edifice, reared its modest head, as if for the " purpose of reminding the spectator, that man had " begun his inroads upon nature, without as yet " taking away from her simplicity and grandeur. I " hardly recollect a scene, which struck me at the " moment more forcibly, or which has left a deeper " or more lasting impression on my memory."

Stark's exact force was three New Hampshire regiments of militia, under the respective commands of Colonels Hubbard, Stickney, and Nichols; a body of militia under Colonel William Williams, from the east side of the mountains; Colonel Herrick's corps of Rangers, formed under the authority of the Vermont Council of Safety; a body of militia from Bennington and vicinity, under Colonel Nathaniel Brush, of which two companies, commanded by Captains Samuel Robinson and Elijah Dewey, were from Bennington, and the force under Colonel Simmons from Berkshire County, making altogether about eighteen hundred men.

The plan of attack as agreed upon by Stark and his officers, and which seems to have been carried out with the greatest attention to detail, was as follows :

Two hundred men, under Colonel Nichols, to take a wide circuit through the woods northward of Baum's redoubt, and gain, undiscovered, a position at the rear of his left. Colonel Herrick's Rangers, together with a part of Colonel Brush's militia from Bennington and vicinity, in all, three hundred men, to take a wide circuit southward, gain a position in the rear of Baum's right, and these two divisions to join and commence the attack. In the mean time, in order to draw the attention of Baum from the concerted movement in his rear, Colonels Hubbard and Stickney were to assume a position before the Tory breastworks, situated on the opposite side of the river at the southward, and one hundred men to march to the front of Baum, to be followed by Stark, with the remainder of the American force, at the proper moment.

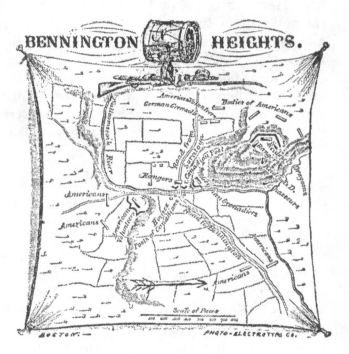

THE BATTLE — FIRST ACTION.

Stark's encampment lay to the eastward of Baum, the Walloomsac flowing between, and bending in such a manner as to necessitate the crossing of it twice in passing directly from one encampment to the other.   Fordable in all places, this did not inconvenience Herrick in his southerly circuit to gain Baum's right, nor any of Stark's troop in marching to the front.

Silas Walbridge, a private in Capt. John Warner's (brother of Seth Warner), company, a part of Herrick's Rangers, says,[1] they went from Stark's encampment, "west across the river, crossed it "again below Sickle's Mills, and came in on the "rear of the Hessian redoubt." Just before reaching the redoubt, "we came in sight of a party of "Indians, and fired on them. They retreated to "the northwest, leaving two killed. Our men "came within ten or twelve rods of the redoubt, "and began firing from behind logs and trees, "and continued firing and advancing until the "Hessians retreated out of their works, and down "the hill to the south. We followed on down "the hill to the level land on the river, and some "pursued on further." Jessie Field, who was in Capt. Dewey's company, which went with Herrick's Rangers, says,[1] "When we came in sight "of the enemy's works, we halted, and it seemed "that the rear of our party had been detained for "some cause. We stood but a short time, when "the firing commenced from the party on the "north. I recollect hearing Lieut. —— exclaim, "'My God, what are we doing? They are killing "our brothers; why are we not ordered to fire?' "In a moment our adjutant came up and ordered "us to advance. We pressed forward, and as the

[1] In a MSS. communication to Hon. Hiland Hall.

"Hessians rose above their works to fire, we dis-
"charged our pieces at them."

After Col. Nichols had gone some little distance,
he sent back to General Stark for a reinforcement
of one hundred men, which were supplied him.

While Colonels Herrick and Nichols were
marching to the rear of the right and left of Baum,
Stark was occupied in diverting the attention of
the Hessians from that movement. "We were
"marched," says Thomas Mellen,[1] of Colonel
Stickney's New Hampshire regiment, "round and
"round a circular hill, till we were tired. Stark
"said it was to amuse the Germans. All the
"while a cannonade was kept up from their breast-
"work. It hurt nobody, and it lessened our fear
"of the great guns. After a while, I was sent
"with twelve others, to lie in ambush on a knoll,
"a little north, and watch for tories on their way
"to join Baum. Presently we saw six coming
"towards us, who, mistaking us for tories, came
"too near us to escape. We disarmed them, and
"sent them, under a guard of three, to Stark.
"While I sat on the hillock, I espied an Indian,
"whom I thought I could kill, and more than
"once cocked my gun, but our orders were not to
"fire. He was cooking his dinner, and now and
"then shot at some of our people."

Stark's stratagem was completely successful in
deceiving Baum himself, although not so his
whole camp. Glick, in his account, remarks, —

---

[1] In an oral statement to Rev. James D. Butler.

" Scouts came in to report that columns of armed
" men were approaching; though whether with
" friendly or hostile intention, neither their ap-
" pearance nor actions enabled our informants to
" ascertain.   It has been stated, that during the
" last day's march our little corps was joined by
" many of the country people; most of whom de-
" manded and obtained arms, as persons friendly
" to the royal cause.   How Col. Baum became so
" completely duped as to place reliance on these
" men I know not; but having listened with com-
" placency to their previous assurances, that in
" Bennington, a large majority of the populace
" were our friends, he was somehow or other per-
" suaded to believe, that the armed bands, of whose
" approach he was warned, were loyalists on
" their way to make tender of their services to the
" leader of the king's troops.   Filled with this
" idea, he despatched positive orders to the out-
" posts, that no molestation should be offered to
" the advancing columns: but that the pickets
" retiring before them should join the main body,
" where every disposition was made to receive
" either friend or foe.   Unfortunately for us, these
" orders were but too faithfully obeyed.   About
" half-past nine o'clock, I, who was not in the
" secret, beheld, to my utter amazement, our ad-
" vanced parties withdraw without firing a shot,
" from thickets which might have been maintained
" for hours against any superiority of numbers;
" and the same thickets occupied by men whose
" whole demeanor, as well as their dress and style
" of equipment, plainly and incontestably pointed
" them out as Americans. . . . . With the solitary
" exception of our leader, there was not a man
" among us who appeared otherwise than satisfied

"that those to whom he had listened were trai-
"tors . . . . He saw no reason to doubt that the
"people, whose approach excited so much appre-
"hension, were the same of whose arrival he had
"been forewarned; and he was prevented from
"placing himself entirely in their power, only by
"the positive refusal of his followers to obey
"orders."

Stark waited patiently for the expected signal
of attack from the rear, and at three o'clock it
came, the scattering reports of firearms from the
direction of Nichols and Herrick announcing that
they had begun the attack.   The welcome sound
sent a thrill through the American ranks, and
with wild hurrahs thus followed their leader and
Warner to the fight.   Before the attack, Stark,
with his sword pointing to the breastworks, said,
MY MEN, THOSE ARE YOUR ENEMIES THE RED-COATS
AND THE TORIES.   WE MUST CONQUER THEM, OR
TO-NIGHT MOLLIE STARK WILL BE A WIDOW! Driv-
ing in the tory out-posts, they crossed the Walloomsac and rushed up the hill.

Herrick's men had met the Indians and driven
them in, in the greatest confusion and wildest
alarm.   Then came the attack on the front.   "We
were surrounded on all sides; columns were advancing everywhere against us," and Baum soon
realized that those whom he had believed as
friends were fast turning into enemies.   A loud
shout from Stark's men in front, in answer to
those from the rear, and then all on to the onset!
The Indians, finding themselves in close quar-

ters and likely soon to be in closer, if they longer
remained, beat a hasty retreat, passing off in single
file as was customary with them, with horrid yells
and the harsh jingling of cow bells. No remon-
strance of Baum's could induce them to remain.
The vacancy in the intrenchments left by them
was filled by one of the field pieces, while the
other was still directed to the front. Baum's men
fought with the desperation of veterans. Repeat-
edly assailed on all sides, they maintained their
ground, trusting that Breyman's troops might
soon reinforce them. Their hopes were fruitless!
Breyman came not; yet they still toiled on, until
at last the solitary tumbril, which contained all of
their spare ammunition, become ignited and blew
up with a violence that seemed to shake the very
ground on which they trod. A momentary lull
in the angry shouts of battle, a temporary cessa-
sion of firing, and then, quickly, cheer upon cheer
from the Americans, as they pushed on to victory.
Rightly guessing the nature of the explosion, they
rushed over the parapet and hand to hand battled
with the foemen. "The bayonet, the butt of the
rifle, the sabre, the pike were in full play; and
men fell, as they rarely fall in modern war, under
the direct blows of their enemies." Such a struggle could not last long. Disheartened and discouraged, Baum's men began to waver. Many of
them wounded and dying, and dead, and many of
them prisoners, the rest surrendered, or sought
safety in flight. But few escaped to tell the story

of their defeat.   Glich, with about thirty others, burst through the American ranks where they appeared to be weakest, and fled, finding a refuge in the depths of the forest.   Colonels Baum and Pfister were both mortally wounded, and were separately borne, the latter a part of the way on the back of Jonathan Armstrong, of Shaftsbury, to a house a mile and a half from the battle-field, where they both died within twenty-four hours.

"Our people behaved with the greatest spirit and bravery imaginable," says Stark, in his official report to the Council of New Hampshire, dated August 18th.   "Had they been Alexanders, or Charleses of Sweden, they could not have behaved better.   The action lasted two hours; at the expiration of which time we forced their breastworks, at the muzzle of their guns."   And then again, in his letter to General Gates, dated at Bennington, August 22nd, he says, "It lasted two hours, the hottest I ever saw in my life — it represented one continual clap of thunder; however, the enemy was obliged to give way, and leave their field-pieces and all their baggage behind them."   The vigor of the Americans in their attack is described by a Hessian eyewitness: "The Americans fought with desperation, pressing within eight paces of the loaded cannon, to take surer aim of the artillerists."

Thus, for the first time in the American Revolution, our soldiers stormed in a regular manner the enemy's fortifications, and as a result their efforts were crowned with victory. It was a victory well earned, and one that only valor and the truest devotion to the cause of Liberty could have won.

THE BATTLE—SECOND ACTION.

At eleven o'clock at night, August 15th, Baum had received a note from Breyman acquainting him with his arrival in the vicinity of Cambridge. Baum at once replied, stating his need for reinforcements, and urging him forward. Upon receiving this early in the morning of the 16th, Breyman at once started, but the artillery horses being very weak, in consequence of not having been fed, as he himself stated, the march progressed but slowly.

Colonel Skeene, the tory royalist, who had been stationed in advance at the St. Coik mill, sent back to Breyman for one officer and twenty men, "as the rebels showed signs of advancing on it." Instead of sending these, Breyman despatched Capt. Gleisenberg ahead, with an advance guard, consisting of sixty grenadiers and chasseurs, and twenty yagers, which he found there undisturbed, on his arrival, at half-past four in the afternoon.

Up to this time Breyman knew nothing of the fate of Baum; nor did Skeene, although he informed him that his force was but two miles distant. With Skeene's advice, Breyman determined to continue his march, and they both set out for Baum's encampment.

After the battle of Hubbardton, Warner's regiment, numbering but one hundred and thirty
men, was stationed at Manchester, twenty miles
north-east of Bennington. It will be remembered
that Stark, upon learning of the advance of the
force under Baum, sent a dispatch to them which
reached its destination on the 14th. Warner
being absent, the command of the regiment de-
volved to Lieutenant-Colonel Samuel Safford.
Safford would have marched at once, but was
prevented from doing so by the absence of Captain John Chipman with a considerable force, who
had gone on a scouting expedition. On the morning of the 15th they set out, and after a long
and weary march, through a drenching rain, every
man wet to the skin, arrived within a mile of Bennington. It was late at night, nearly midnight,
says one who was with them, when they reached
this place, and the arms and ammunition having
been so long exposed to the inclement weather
that they occupied a considerable portion of the
next day's forenoon in preparing for action. Ammunition, too, was not at all plenty, and this
might have detained them a little longer. At all
events it was about noon, or a little after, when
they marched through Bennington village on
their way to the battle-field.

Stark, in his order issued previous to the first
action, had guaranteed the soldiers whatever they
might capture. "I promised in my order," he
says in his letter to Gates, "that the soldiers

should have all the plunder taken in the enemy's camp," and so when the few men Baum had left, gave way and retreated, with the exception of those who surrendered, many of the Americans scattered over the field in search of desirable property, while others, worn out and exhausted, sought the most convenient place for rest. Guards had also been dispatched with the prisoners for Bennington, and consequently when the word came that a fresh body of the enemy was in the immediate vicinity, confusion in Stark's ranks was almost complete. However, by the combined personal exertions of the officers a sufficient force was mustered to make a fair show of numbers, and these were ordered into line of battle.

Breyman had now arrived in sight, and observing a considerable body of armed men, some in blouses and some in jackets, hastening towards an eminence on his left flank, called Colonel Skinner's attention to it. That worthy royalist felt satisfied these were friends, and so rode towards them, and calling out, received for a reply a volley that quickly convinced him of his error. Breyman then ordered one battalion to assail the height, while the yagers and grenadiers advanced on the right.

Stark, almost discouraged in his attempts to rally the troops, was on the point of ordering a retreat, when Warner rode forth, and exclaimed, "Stand to it, my lads: you shall have help im-"mediately." The enemy pressed close, and the

Americans were on the point of yielding ground, when the news came that Warner's regiment was close at hand. An orderly sergeant,[1] who acted in this regiment, thus relates their advance.

"We now began to meet the wounded. . . . .
"Here I was put in command of the left flank
"guard, and the march was continued by the regi-
"ment down the road, and by myself and guard
"across the flat. There was also a flank guard
"on the right. We continued our march until
"we came to the top of the eminence, . . . where
"I found the regiment had halted. On inquiring
"the cause, I was told that a reinforcement of the
"enemy was near. I mounted a fence, and saw
"the enemy's flank guard beyond the next hill,
"say half a mile distant. We were then ordered
"to form a line for battle, by filing to the right;
"but, owing to the order not being understood in
"the rear, the line was formed by filing to the left,
"which brought many of our men into a sort of
"swamp, instead of on the hill above, where we
"should have been. We, however, waited the ap-
"proach of the enemy, and commenced firing as
"they came up; but owing, as I think, to the un-
"favorable nature of the ground, we soon began
"a retreat, which was continued slowly and in
"good order, firing constantly for about three-
"quarters of a mile, until we reached the high
"ground, west of the run of water, where we made
"a stand. The enemy had two pieces of cannon
"in the road, and their line extended a considera-
"ble distance both below and above the road. A
"party of Hessians undertook to outflank us on
"the right, and partly succeeded, but were finally

[1] Jacob Safford, in a communication to Hon. Hiland Hall.

"repulsed and driven back. The action was warm
"and close for nearly two hours, when it being near
"dark, the enemy were forced to retreat.

Although Warner's regiment arrived fresh and
in high spirits, yet the vigorous attack of Breyman
seemed at one time to be carrying the day. His
two pieces of cannon, stationed advantageously,
had continued a fire of grape shot, clearing a way
for the Hessians to advance. Stark used the two
cannon taken from Baum, with considerable effect,
restraining the enemy, until his own men might
gain time to make a solid defense.

Breyman's ammunition at last giving out, his
cannon ceased firing, which so encouraged our
men, that they rushed on with renewed life.
Breyman endeavored, in vain, to save his field-
pieces; they fell into the hands of the Americans,
and then the fortunes of the day turned. The
enemy retreated on every side, leaving their dead,
and many of their wounded on the field. The
Americans pursued, but darkness setting in, many
of them escaped. "Had daylight lasted one hour
"longer," says Stark, "we should have taken the
"whole body of them." The struggle ended at
Sancoik Mill, Stark hesitating to pursue farther,
for the fear of killing some of his own men in the
darkness.

After five hours of severe fighting, the Americans were rewarded with victory; most gloriously
had the day been won!

The Americans captured in this battle, four brass field-pieces, four ammunition wagons, twelve brass barrelled drums, seven hundred stand of arms, several Hessian swords, and a number of horses, carriages, etc.   Six hundred and fifty-four prisoners were taken, two hundred and seven killed, and eighty wounded, making the enemy's total loss to amount to nine hundred and forty-one in killed, wounded, and prisoners.   Our loss, according to Stark, "was inconsiderable ; about "forty wounded, and thirty killed." Stark lost his horse, saddle, and bridle, in the action.

Of the cannon captured, two are now in the State House at Montpelier.

One Hessian gun and bayonet, one broadsword, one brass barrelled drum, and one grenadier's cap, of the captured trophies, were presented to each of the states of Vermont, New Hampshire, and Massachusetts.

STARK'S LETTER ACCOMPANYING THE GIFTS TO MASSACHUSETTS.

"BENNINGTON, September 15, 1777.

"General Stark begs leave to present to the "State of the Massachusetts Bay, and pray their "acceptance of the same, one Hessian gun and "bayonet, one broadsword, one brass barrelled " drum, and one grenadier's cap, taken from the "enemy, in the memorable battle, fought at Wal-"loomsac, on the 16th of August last; and requests "that the same may be kept in commemoration "of that glorious victory, obtained over the enemy "that day, by the united troops of that State, "those of New Hampshire, and Vermont, which "victory ought to be kept in memory, and handed "down to futurity, as a lasting and laudable ex- "ample for the sons and daughters of the victors, "in order never to suffer themselves to become "the prey of those mercenary tyrants and syco- "phants, who are daily endeavoring to ruin and "destroy us."

Massachusetts, in accepting the trophies, replied as follows :

"BOSTON, 12*th of December*, 1777.

"SIR,—The General Assembly of this state, take "the earliest opportunity, to acknowledge the re- "ceipt of your acceptable present,—the tokens of "victory at the memorable battle of Bennington.

"The events of that day strongly mark the "bravery of the men, who, unskilled in war, forced "from their intrenchments, a chosen number of "veteran troops, of boasted Britons ; as well as "the address and valor of the General, who di- "rected their movements, and led them on to con- "quest. This signal exploit opened the way to a "rapid succession of advantages, most important "to America.

"These trophies shall be safely deposited in the "archives of the State, and there remind posterity "of the irresistible power of the God of armies, "and the honors due to the memory of the brave.

"Still attended with like successes, may you long "enjoy the just rewards of a grateful country."

Vermont's acknowledgment.

"*State of Vermont, in Council of Safety,* "BENNINGTON, 20*th Sept.* 1777.

"The Council beg leave to return their sincere

"thanks to the Hon. Brigadier-Gen. John Stark,
"for the infinite service he has been pleased to
"do them, in defending them and their constitu-
"ents, from the cruelty and bloody rage of our
"unnatural enemy, who sought our destruction
"on the 16th of August last. They also return
"their grateful acknowledgments for the honor
"the General has been pleased to do the council,
"by presenting them with one Hessian gun, with
"a bayonet, one broadsword, one brass barrelled
"drum, and a grenadier's cap, taken on the mem-
"orable 16th of August, for the use of this State.
"The General may rely upon it, they will be re-
"served for the use they were designed.

 " I am, dear General, with sentiments of esteem,
        "your most obedient humble servant,
            "THOMAS CHITTENDEN, *President.*
"HON. BRIG.-GEN. STARK."

Stark also presented to the Vermont Council
of Safety, a Hessian broadsword, as a mark of
his approbation of their zeal in the public cause.

        "*In Council of Safety,* 6th Sept. 1777.
 "The Council's Compliments most cordially
"wait on his honor, Brigadier-General Stark, with
"their sincere thanks, for the honor the General
"has been pleased to do them, by presenting them
"with a *Hessian broadsword,* taken by a number
"of troops from the State of New Hampshire,
"and elsewhere, under his immediate command,
"in the memorable battle, fought in Walloomsack,
"near this place, on the 16th of August last; and
"also for the honor the General has been pleased
"to do them, in applauding their exertions in a
"public weal, as a Council.   JOSEPH FAY, *Sec'y.*"

    "BRIG.-GEN. STARK."

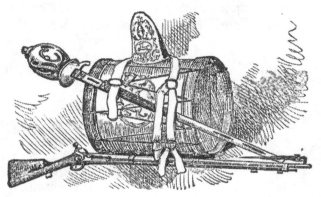

TROPHIES OF THE BATTLE OF BENNINGTON.

The comparative strength of forces can never be accurately known. Stark had under his command, most likely, between seventeen hundred and eighteen hundred men; but they were mostly what might be termed raw militia, who not only worked under the disadvantage of no experience, or but very little, but also, without full and complete equipments, as possessed by the enemy. Baum had nearly six hundred men, not counting his Indian allies, which were an hundred and fifty more. Breyman, without doubt, had a thousand men; and so, as nearly as we can determine, the forces were not far from being equal. Possibly the Americans were a little the stronger, to the amount of Warner's regiment, but the enemy's superior military equipments and knowledge more than offset this number. The only way to account for our victory on that day is to attribute

it to the superior tact of our officers, and the
hardy valor and determined bravery of our men.

OFFICIAL REPORT OF GENERAL STARK TO THE NEW HAMPSHIRE COUNCIL

"BENNINGTON, *August* 13*th*, 1777.

"Gentlemen,—I congratulate you on the late
"success of your troops under my command, by
"express. I propose to give you a brief account of
"my proceedings, since I wrote to you last.

"I left Manchester, Vt., on the 8th instant, and
"arrived here on the 9th. The 13th I was in-
"formed that a party of Indians were at Cam-
"bridge, which is twelve miles distant from this
"place, on their march thither. I detached Col.
"Gregg, with two hundred men under his com-
"mand, to stop their march.

"In the evening, I had information by express,
"that there was a large body of the enemy on their
"way, with field-pieces, in order to march through
"the country, commanded by Governor Skeene.
"The 14th, I marched with my brigade, and a
"portion of the State militia, to oppose them, and
"cover Gregg's retreat, who found himself unable
"to withstand their superior numbers. About
"four miles from this town, I accordingly met
"him on his return, and the enemy in close pur-
"suit of him, within a half mile of his rear; but
"when they discovered me, they presently halted
"on a very advantageous piece of ground.

"I drew up my little army, on an eminence in
"view of their encampment, but could not bring
"them to an engagement. I marched back about
"a mile, and there encamped. I sent a few men
"to skirmish with them, who killed thirty of them,

"with two Indian chiefs. The 15th it rained all
"day: I sent out parties to harrass them.

"The 16th, I was joined by this State's (Vt.)
"militia, and those of Berkshire county. I divided
"my army into three divisions, and sent Lieut.
"Col. Nichols, with two hundred and fifty¹ men on
"the rear of their left wing, Colonel Herrick on the
"rear of their right, ordered, when joined, to attack
"the same. In the meantime, I sent three hun-
"dred men to oppose the enemy's front, to draw
"their attention that way. Soon after, I detached
"Colonels Hubbard and Stickney on their right
"wing, with two hundred men, to attack that part;
"all which plans had their desired effect. Colonel
"Nichols sent me word that he stood in need of
"a reinforcement, which I readily granted, con-
"sisting of one hundred men; at which time he
"commenced the attack, precisely at three o'clock
"in the afternoon, which was followed by all the
"rest. I pushed forward the remainder with all
"speed.

"Our people behaved with the greatest spirit
"and bravery imaginable. Had they been Alex-
"anders or Charleses of Sweden, they could not
"have behaved better.

"The action lasted two hours; at the expira-
"tion of which time we forced their breastworks,
"at the muzzle of their guns; took two pieces of
"brass cannon, with a number of prisoners; but
"before I could get them into proper form again,
"I received intelligence that there was a large re-
"inforcement within two miles of us, on their
"march, which occasioned us to renew our attack;
"but, luckily for us, Colonel Warner's regiment
"came up, which put a stop to their career. We

¹ In a letter to Gates, written four days later, Stark says two hundred men.

"soon rallied, and in a few minutes, the action
"began very warm and desperate, which lasted
"until night. We used their cannon against them,
"which proved of great service to us.

"At sunset, we obliged them to retreat a sec-
"ond time; we pursued them till dark, when I
"was obliged to halt, for fear of killing our men.

"We recovered two pieces more of their can-
"non, together with all their baggage, a number
"of horses, carriages, etc.; killed upwards of two
"hundred of the enemy in the field of battle.

"The number of wounded is not yet known, as
"they are scattered about in many places. I have
"one lieutenant colonel, since dead, (Colonel
"Baum), one major, seven captains, fourteen
"lieutenants, four ensigns, two cornets, one judge
"advocate, one baron, two Canadian officers, six
"sergeants, one aid-de-camp, one Hessian chaplain,
"three Hessian surgeons, and seven hundred pris-
"oners.

"I enclose you a copy of General Burgoyne's
"instructions to Colonel Baum, who commanded
"the detachment that engaged us. Our wounded
"are forty-two, ten privates, and four officers, be-
"longing to my brigade; one dead. The dead
"and wounded in the other corps, I do not know,
"as they have not brought in their returns yet.

"I am, Gentlemen, with the greatest regard,
"your most obedient and humble servant,

"JOHN STARK, *Brigadier General Commanding.*

"P. S. I think in this action, we have returned
"the enemy a proper compliment for their Hub-
"bardston engagement."

Congress, upon learning of Stark's victory at
Bennington, hastened to make up for their neglect

of his talents as a military leader, by making him a Brigadier-General in the army of the United States. Massachusetts voted him "a complete suit of clothes becoming his rank, together with a piece of linen." Everywhere people were loud in in his praise. The man who had been so long neglected and forgotten; the man who had been laughed and sneered at, as not capable of commanding anything more than a regiment, was suddenly discovered to possess a military ability of essential importance to the country!

Was Col. Warner in the First Action?

I answer at once, yes, although on turning to the pages of many of our National, and some of our State Historians, we are led to believe that he arrived with his regiment in time to meet Breyman's reinforcements. That Warner's regiment arrived at that time, there is no reason to doubt. That Warner came with them, is a mistake. Hildreth, in his History of the United States, says, "Warner's regiment luckily arrived at the same time," meaning at the moment of Breyman's arrival; nothing about Warner being there before then. Bancroft, in his History of the United States: "Warner now first brought up his regiment." Marshall in his Life of Washington: "Fortunately at this critical juncture, Colonel Warner came up with his continental regiment." Irving, in his Life of Washington: "Colonel Seth Warner's corps fortunately arrived from Bennington."

Nothing about Warner's being there previously. Botta's American Revolution: "Colonel Warner arrived at the head of his regiment." Ira Allen's History of Vermont: "At this critical moment, Col. Warner arrived with his regiment." Samuel Williams's History of Vermont: "Colonel Warner came up with his regiment from Manchester."

Warner was with Stark several days previous to, and during the entire 16th of August. When Stark first learned of the advance of the enemy in force, he, to use his own words, "sent to Manchester, to Colonel Warner's regiment, that was stationed there," as well as to the militia in the surrounding neighborhood. "I then," he says, "marched in company with Warner, Williams, Herrick, and Brush, with all the men that were present." When Breyman arrived, and seemed about to turn the fortunes of the day, Stark says, "Luckily for us, that moment Colonel Warner's *regiment* came up fresh." Still farther along in his letter to Gates: "Colonel Warner's superior skill in the action was of extraordinary service to me." In his official reports to the Council of New Hampshire, he also speaks of Colonel Warner's *regiment* as coming up in time to put a stop to the enemy's career.

Daniel Chipman, in his Life of Warner, admits that he might have been with Stark just previous to the battle, but thinks he must have gone back to get his regiment, Stark delaying the action until he should arrive, and getting impatient at

three o'clock, commencing the attack. That Stark
having nearly eighteen hundred men, should wait
hours for one hundred and thirty more, before at-
tacking a force of six or seven, or even eight hundred, is simply absurd. Stark, in his letter to
Gates, explains the delay: "I pursued my plan,
"detached Col. Nichols, with two hundred men,
"to attack them in the rear; I also sent Colonel
"Herrick, with three hundred men, in the rear of
"their right, both to join, *and when joined, to at-*
"*tack their rear.* . . . About three o'clock we got
"all ready for the attack. Col. Nichols begun
"the same, which was followed by all the rest."
That don't seem to indicate that he was waiting
for Warner.

Thomas Mellen, in a statement given to Rev.
Mr. Butler, says, "Stark and Warner rode up
"near the enemy, to reconnoitre; were fired at
"with the cannon, and came galloping back.
"Stark rode with shoulder's bent forward, and
"cried out to his men: 'Those rascals know that
"I am an officer; don't you see they honor me
"with a big gun as a salute?'"

Solomon Safford, who turned out with Captain
Samuel Robinson's company, says,[1] "On the morn-
"ing of the battle, after the company had started
"off with Col. Herrick, Gen. Stark and Col. War-
"ner rode past him on horseback, and accosted
"him."

Rev. Isaac Jeninngs, in his Memorials of a Cen-

[1] MSS. statement to Hon. Hiland Hall.

tury, says, "William Carpenter of Swansea, N. H., so his son, Judge Carpenter, of Akron, Ohio, told me, used to relate, as what he himself heard, that the order was given by Gen. Stark to an aid, to retreat.   Warner heard it, and said, 'Stand to it, my lads; you shall have help immediately,'" meaning, of course, his own regiment.   This was immediately after the first action.

Other proofs might be cited, but it is not necessary.   Sufficient have been given, to convince any reasonable mind, anxious for the truth.   Let us trust future historians, when writing of the Battle of Bennington, may be more careful in rendering " honor to whom honor is due."

Anecdotes and Individual Experiences.

One venerable old man had five sons in the battle.   As might naturally be supposed, he awaited, with anxiety, the results of the contest. At last news came, but the messenger who brought it, brought with him, also, tidings for the father, that he feared would fill the old man's heart with grief.   As gently as possible, he told him he had something bad to tell him, concerning one of his sons.

" Did he disobey orders, or desert his post ? " he asked.

" No."

" Did he falter in the charge ? "

" No, worse than that ! "

" What then, worse than that ? "

"He is dead!" was the answer.

"Then it is not worse," exclaimed the father. " Bring him in, that I may once more gaze on the face of my darling boy." And when they brought him in, covered with dust and blood, he called for water and sponge, and with his own hand bathed the disfigured features, declaring, at the same time, that he had never experienced a more glorious or happier day in his life.

Rev. Thomas Allen, of the Berkshire militia, fought as a private, and was among the foremost to advance on the Hessian's defense. Arriving within speaking distance, he mounted a stump, and called out to them to surrender, and thereby save the effusion of blood. A volley was the only reply, which, the reverend gentleman escaping, he returned to the ranks. Here, finding himself a better marksman than his brother, who was also present, he said to him, "Joe, you load and I'll fire," and so they worked together, side by side, until the last grand charge that carried Baum's works. In after years he delighted to recall the scenes incidental to that glorious day. In conversation, some one asked if he killed anybody on that occasion.

"I don't exactly know that I killed any one," was the reply, "nor indeed how near I came to it. " It was just this way; off some distance, I observed "a clump of bushes, from which arose, every now " and then, a little cloud of smoke, preceded by a " momentary flash, and the sharp report of a gun.

"I noticed too, that one of our men fell, either
"wounded or dead, every time this phenomenon
"occurred, so I naturally concluded that some-
"thing was wrong for our side.   I loaded up very
"carefully, and fired into the midst of that clump
"of bushes.   I am not certain, mind you, that I
"did really *kill* any one ; *but I know I put out that*
"*flash!*"

This was a proud day, said one old soldier, in
his reminiscences of the battle, quoting nearly his
own words, — this was a proud day for the poor
Green Mountain Boys, who were yet smarting
with the wounds they had so lately received at
the downfall of Ticonderoga.   They could not
readily forget the slaughter of their brothers of
Colonel Warner's regiment, that was so badly cut
to pieces at Hubbardtown ; and when the word
came, when the alarm sounded that the enemy
were coming, every man left his plow and his axe,
and forthwith marched to meet the invaders, and
drive them from the field.   They marched, some
of them with officers, many of them without;
there was no anxiety as to who should command,
indeed little thought was given as to whether
there should be any commander, the principal
idea being to gain a good position, and with careful aim, bring down the invaders, one by one.

Stark ordered a Colonel with his regiment, to
reinforce one of the wings, that had sustained considerable loss in the action.   The Colonel marched
at the instant, but with a certain step peculiar to

himself, slow, firm, and steady. The whole parish was in his regiment, and they had brought with them their much-loved parson, without whose blessing, they could scarcely think to prosper. The officer in command of the corps to be relieved, fearing every instant, his men, from fatigue and loss, would give way, sent to hasten the Colonel. "Tell them," said he, "we're coming," and kept his pace steadily on. This man was, at home, a deacon.—wore an old-fashioned, long-waisted coat, with large pocket-flaps, and herring-boned cuffs, and a three cornered hat, the fore-part something resembling the handle of a pipkin, except that the extreme point of it might have endangered the eye of a mosquito, had he run unguardedly against it.

A second express arrived. "Colonel, for God's sake hurry; my men are beginning to fall back!" "That will make room for us,—tell 'em we're coming," keeping still the unaltered pace and phiz quite placid and unconcerned.

A third message was treated just as cool. Soon they emerged from behind a coppice, in full view of the enemy, and several balls passed over them. "Halt," said the Colonel, "form column, and let us attend to prayers." The chaplain was called, and ordered, with all due formality, to attend to his duty, but during this solemnity, an unlucky shot wounded one of the men. The Colonel now, for the first time, began to show some little impatience, for no sooner had the parson pronounced

"Amen," than the men were ordered to march. But yet the Colonel kept his steady pace, until he had taken the ground in front of the poor fellows who were almost ready to leave the field, and but for the love of Liberty, could not have kept it half so long. And then the word came from the Colonel, "Give it to 'em, give it to 'em!" and he stepped along the ranks calmly as ever, chewing his quid, which he now and then replaced, often obliging those who stood next to him with his box. "The Hessians are in front," said he, our wives and children in the rear. Liberty is the prize,— we fight for Liberty!" The enemy pressed, but pressed on to their destruction. We fought, we bled, and we conquered.

CPSIA information can be obtained
at www.ICGtesting.com
Printed in the USA
BVHW080033090221
599628BV00002B/265

9 780548 466612